AF570740

PILLS TO PURGE
THE PAINES OF LOVE

ARIEL HALL

With Twenty-six Drawings by the Author

BOSTON
BRANDEN PRESS
PUBLISHERS

Printed in the United States of America
Library of Congress Catalog Card Number 74-83065
ISBN 0-8283-1591-4

CONTENTS

A DIALOGUE BETWEEN THE AUTHOR AND THE PRINTER

Printer: Good Morrow, Sir, Pray enter and tell me thy Businesse.

Author: P—Pills—Pills—

Printer: PILLS?—but I have not call'd a Physitian

Author: Pills to purge—a Booke, Sir, I am the author of a Booke.

Printer: What title do you design to give this booke?

Author: PILLS to Purge the Paines of Love; or, PILLS to Preserve Love's Pleasures. The title signifies little or nothing.

Printer: Then I am like to make a very hopeful bargain this morning; you would have me take on this batch of pills for a condition we know is not to be purg'd or preserv'd?

Author: Tush! Tush! Hold thy temper. I do no worse than all the Astrologers and Divines who prate about compatibility, sexual inadequacy, impotence, frigidity, and so on. These Love-Quacks who exalt Celestiall Beds and who imploy Whores to advertise their wares are no better than my simple Specifics. I inquire into the Cause, Nature, and Value of things.

Printer: I am, Sir, in this point, a Quaker, and I will not willingly be convinc'd. Pray tell me—am I oblig'd to advertise your useless physic?

Author: I beleeve, Sir, it will increase your fame, for it has already cur'd the paines of many of those unfortunates who suffer this disease.

Printer: Why then, do you put over the door, that the Pills signify "Little or Nothing?" It is a strange sort of information to get customers by.

Author: I will gladly tell you some of the reasons; first, the natural inquisitive humour that reigns in all mankind after Novelty; for no sooner will the title be read, but the reader will query what it is about,—conclude it some maggot or other, and to be satisfied, will buy it. Then, I have known many dull books that have sold well by the aid of an ingeniose title: such as *A Tale in a Tub*, or *A Way to get Wealth*, or *A Passage to the Moon*. Such an advertisement as "PILLS" that are guaranteed to cure some disease or other will always appeal to the credulous, even though the Pills be but airy concoctions, and the disease, hopeless.

Printer: I am mightily obliged to you, Sir, for the method you have taken to expose me to ridicule. Hand me your scribblings; if your whim does not take, I will never buy goods again before I have sampled the contents.

Domestick cares afflict the Husband's bed
or paines his head;
Those that live single take it for a curse
or doe things worse.
Some would have children; those that have them mone,
or wish them gone.
What is it then, to have, or have no wife
but single thraldome, or a double strife?

Sir Francis Bacon

An Appel a Daye keeps the Doctor awaye,
So the Serpente told her and she did tell him
This advyce was the cause of Originall Sinne.

THE BEGINNING of THE END

"It is not good for Man to be alone," sayd God Almighty as He surveyed His Creation. He had completed the Firmament, which He call'd Heaven, and the Dry Land, which He call'd Earth. He gazed on the gathering together of the waters, which He call'd the Seas; He consider'd the two wonderful great lights: the greater golden light which He call'd the Sun, and the lesser silver light which He call'd the Moon. He survey'd the skies with their clouds and small stars. He rejoic'd in the seasons, with the fruits, flowers and herbes most timely to them, also various beastes, fishes and fowle for pleasure and sustenance. Man was His last creation, but he had no mate, so God created Woeman, who was to be a helper to the man, not a hinderer; a companion for his comforte; more than a friend and less than a trouble. He gave them names—Adam and Eve He call'd them, and placed them in a garden where were alle things for their pleasure. God warn'd them only that they must never eat of the fruit of the Appel-tree which stood in the midst of the garden, lest they die.

The serpente, who had been eaves-dropping, sayd they would not die at all, but onlie be as gods. So Eve tempted Adam with the fruit, and having once tasted it, his appetite grew. When, in the evening, God call'd to Adam, Adam did not at first answer; he was ashamed because he was naked. "How didst thou know this?"

asked God, "hast thou eaten of the forbidden fruit?" Adam sayd that Eve had given him to eat of the appel which had been commended to her by the serpente. For this disobedience God cast them out of the garden; in their nakedness and shame they made themselves breeches from figge leaves.

"Increase and multiply," sayd God as they departed; but many have since misunderstood this commandment, for God requires children, not bastards.

In the early seventeenth century there has been so great a demand for Bibles that they have been printed everywhere, from Edinburgh to Amsterdam; often they are filled with mistakes, as the famous Bible which left out the NOT in the seventh commandment. This Bible is quite popular and is much preferred by the congregations that use it. The book of Common Prayer also is so poorly printed as to be quite illegible, but the printer declared it made no difference since people should have the prayers by heart anyway. By all this have many innocent people (particularly the young) been led astray.

The very word "Marriage" portends a Merry-age, yet this is not a deed to be danc'd into lightlie. In choosing a wife, a man should seek one of a sober, mild aspect, with courteous behaviour, a steady eye and an even gait. He ought also to regard the education and quality of his choice, for love looks sometimes with the mind as well as with the eye. After this, take a little glance backwards at the stock: if men be so careful to have their horses and cows of a good breed, how much more should they their wives, from whom they expect to preserve their own images and virtues.

Diogenes was once ask'd, what time of a man's life was best to marry. "In youth," he sayd, "it is too soon. In age, it is too late." He insinuated thereby that it was best never. In the opinion of most woemen, a man without a wife is but "Misery in apparel." Whosoever thou art, that would'st for freedom adventure bondage, know that every good woeman makes not for every man a good wife; no otherwise than every good dish digests with every stomach. Marriage hath many paines, but celibacy hath no pleasures.

A learned man hath sayd that, in his opinion, both Man and Woeman bear Paine and Sorrow (and for aught he knew—Pleasure too) best in a horizontal position.

WHAT IS LOVE?

Love is certainly, at least alphabetically speaking, one of the most:

A gitating
B edazzling
C ontumacious
D ecumbent affairs of life—the most
E xasperating
F labbergasting
G oddaming
H abituating
I mpudicitous (if you don't know this, look it up)
J igumbobing
K icksie-wicksieish
L overly of all human passions, at the same time, the most
M elliferous
N ose-bagging
O rgulous
P iscatorial (yes, it has something to do with fishing)
R idiculous
S crumptious—

In short 'tis of such nature, as I told my uncle Pliny, one Sunday afternoon, that you can scarce combine two ideas together upon it without an arsy-versy. "What's that?" cried my Uncle Pliny.

"It's a word of contrary opinion, covering everything from front to back and back to front, but no longer used in polite society," I replied.

"Then why use it?" asked my uncle Pliny.

"No reason," I answered, "except that I do not intend to be polite."

. . . A delicate balancing act . . .

A MAN AND TWO WOEMEN

A Man which has two Woemen on the String must balance himself verie carefullie, especially if one of these be his Wyfe. Should he lean too far in one direction, one Woeman or the Other is left up in the aire. He must take care that the Wyfe, on one side, be ignorant of the Wench on the other. This is tiresome work and it is a brave man who attempts it for long without losing his balance.

Aesop tells of a middle-aged man who took a phansy to marrie two wives, of an age one under the other. They both took extreemely good care of him and both lov'd him dearly. Each one would comb her good man's head in the morning and each would pluck out here and there a Haire, so as to make it all of the same Colour. The older Wyfe, she pluck'd out all the brown haires; the younger wyfe, she pluck'd out all the white haires—so, between them, at the conclusion, they left him no better than a Buzzard.

Manie Birdes and Beastes take but one Mate and this is sayd to be the Law of God. It is not always the Nature of Man but it has manie Advantages.

Ariel Hale.

GRANDMA KNOWS BEST

It is of little use to preach Philosophie to the young, thought Grandma sadly; and Logick does but curdle a Virgin's milk. Young mayds of these dayes, who lie alone in their bedds onlie muse how they may lose their long-kept mayden-heads. She was reading to her Grandaughter from an ancient booke of wisdome containing such wise precepts as:

Sheep's cloathing oft conceals a Wolf.
As soon goes the young sheep to the pot as the old.
Don't leape over the stile before you come at it.
A beard on the chin hides manie a sin.

"Now tis goode to hold a candle before the devil," sayd the old ladie, "I know, because I have been through the matrimonial oven severall times myself. But I must give you one more bit of advyce. Should you experience any little aberrations in domestic felicity, just remember to kiss your husband Good Night. It works like a charm. Faith! In these days a maydenhead stands like a game at Pell-Mell; if the ball fits into the hole, all's well; if not—Farewell alle."

God 'a Mercy, Wench; Bear and Forbear
Be lowly, not sullen, if aught go amiss
What wrestling may lose thee, that win with a kiss.

THE TRAGICALL STORIE OF JOSEPHINE LACKWIT

Wherein it is shewn that nothing is more capable of troubling our Reason and consuming our Health, than secret Notions of Jealousie in Solitude

JOSEPHINE

A Young Asse call'd Josephine made her home since the day of her birth with Farmer and Mistress Lackwit who dwelt near Broad Oak in Sussex. She was a comelie young asse, mightilie spoyl'd by the good Farmer and fancied herself to be alone in his affections. He came everie morning to her stall with a bit of sugar or an appel; pull'd her eares and sometimes kiss'd her nose, saying "How doth my sweet Josephine today?" The heart of the young asse swell'd with the pleasant emotion of love and she thought, "How happie am I to have this deare friende."

But the worlde seldom stays the same and tryalls and troubles often come when least expected. One day a beautifull new Ponie was ledd into the stall by Farmer Lackwit. Josephine perceived that she was not nearly so comelie nor was she so tallented to learn the little tricks and devices that Farmer Lackwit taught the new ponie; she grew verie unhappy in her minde as well as jealous in her heart. "I will stay here no longer," she thought, "I will run away; I will find a new home."

So she did one dark night. Sometime later she found herself in the barn of another farmer, not so kind as the first. Some dayes later she was visited by Farmer Lackwit, but Josephine bit and kicked—she would not listen to wisdome. He reminded her that good words cost nought; ill words corrupt good manners. A friend, my dear Josephine, is not so soon gotten as lost, he reminded her. Haste makes waste, he sayd; Maids that wear cork shoes oft step awry. Ye have been like the cow that gives a good sop of milk and then casts it down with her owne heeles. May God send you rest and a peck of fleas in your nest. Adew, Josephine. Adew.

MUSITIANS, PAINTERS, WRITERS, PLAYERS, DANCERS

A Gentleman of my acquaintance has call'd to my attention the analogy between practitioners of the arts and those who embark on the voyage of Matrimony. "Should those who marry," he remarked to me over a glass of ale at The Mermaid, "seek to perfect the amenities of this estate no more than one quarter so much as do those who would master a Viol da Gamba the condition of Matrimonie would greatly benefit thereby."

I shall enlarge upon this thought and suggest that these are people from whom we can learn much and profit from their devotion to an Ideal of Perfection. For are not all of us Players here on Earth, and is not all the World a stage?

Musitians must everlastinglie practice to make perfect and must obey the laws of Harmonie. They must play together; not everie man in his own way and at his own tempo, and not out of tune with his neighbor. There is one Director for them in an orchestra, whom they must follow; as there is but one Director for us. It is all for God's Glory and Pleasant Recreation, said Papa Bach, for without these objects there is no true music, but only an infernal scraping and bawling.

Painters look at nature to create a new beauty; their visions are an eternal joy to others, dependent on the quality of their inner eye; yet,—they needed patience to learn the craft. Players and Dancers must likewise train their bodies and minds, seeking, like all artists: truth, simplicity, mystery and perfection. Constant striving lies behind their inspiration, for art is a life and life is an art to be lived and shared with others.

"Man was not created to be an idle fellow," wrote Sir Thomas Dekker in his *Seven Deadlie Sinnes*; "he was made for other purpose than to be ever eating as swine, ever sleeping as dormice, ever dumb as the fishes in the sea, or ever prating to no purpose as the birdes of the ayre. He was not set down in the universal orchard to stand still as a tree, and so to be cut down, but to be cut down if he should stand still."

When we consider how truly marvellous and wonderful are the works of men, when they will work together under God's guidance; so can the state of Matrimonie be a noble creation when its Foundation is laid with Cooperation; its Design made harmonious with Discipline; its Hearth made warm with Unselfishness; its Walls adorned with Pleasant Graces; its Windows open to God; and its Roof covered with Love.

LUCKY STARRS, COLOURS AND TALISMANS

On my Travells through Ireland, I once met with an olde Romany pedler, who read my Fortune by the Starrs. He told me manie things having to do with Magick, which, to my surprize, he sayd was FAITH.

Thus, Friday is a lucky day for Marriage, because that is the day that Adam united with Eve.

The Aquamarine, the Emeralde, Ruby, Topaz and black-lined Turquoise are stones that produce love and affection.

Blew is the Colour to wear for Success in any greatt Undertaking. Greene, when seeking Favours. Cerise, when hoping to attract the opposite Sexe.

Colours have Sounds, he tolde me, and sounds have vibrations and numbers; and with Numbers we can reach the Starrs. All proceed from the number One, which signifies Unitie. All are part of One, and All return to One.

As Breath is Life, he spoke of breathing exercises for everie part of the Bodie, and particularlie for Health and Success. The Breathings must be accompnied by Affirmations. These Beliefs are more ancient than Astrologie.

Goodnesse is an Actual Shielde against Evill, he sayd. Love is the greattest Magnetique Force in the Universe. Faith in Self (God) can produce marvellous Results; for when the Mind of Man is joined with the Mind of God there is wonderful Virtue in a Worke.

There are Starrs in the Depths of the Sea, and Starrs at the Top of the Heavens, and we must know Both. Man is a Sun, Moon and Heaven filled with Starrs, he sayd to me.

Ariel Hall

THE CELESTIAL BEDD

There was not long ago invented and displayed a Celestial Bedd by a man whose name I have forgot. This bedd has since been suppressed and forbidden by Parliament as being injurious to the Public Morals, and more's the pittie, for the purpose of this bedd was to distract from the Monotonie of Sexe and to prove false the old saying that a man looks "with Rapture on a Woman onlie twice,—once on her Bridall Bedd and again on her Death Bedd." Nontheless there has been a Great Decay in the public Morals and we have not the Celestial Bedd to blame.

Now in these days we have manie sorts of bedds: fethyr (feather) bedds and wool-sack bedds, truckle bedds and bundle bedds, convex bedds and concave bedds, single bedds and double bedds, as well as some bedds that will accomodate four couples at a time, which can be found at some Inns. The word "Bedd" derives from a prehistoric Aryan word "bhodh" and meant "to dig." Be that as it may, a bedd is a necessary piece of furnishing and is oft passed on from father to son. When used for sleep a bedd is usually horizontal, but for love it is not necessarilly so, nor is it indispensable. If we learn of Sexe from the birds, the bees and the beastes, wrote Sir Thomas Browne in *Vulgar Errors,* we find there is not one, but manie ways of Coition according to the divers shapes and conformations. Thus some unite laterallie, or sidewise, as Worms; some circularly, as Serpentes; some pronely, as Apes, Procupines and Hedgehoggs; some mixtly (that is, the male ascending the female) as most Quadrupedds; some aversely, as all Crustaceous Animals, and also Retromingents, as Panthers, Tygers and Hares.

The ways of Man are to seek Diversitie and what gives one pleasure is so apt to give the other. A young lady of Queen Elizabeth's Court has recently been relieved of her distress on the Terrace at Whitehall Palace; a chambermaid likewise against a tree in St. Paul's Churchyard when returning from a play. There are those who prefer to stand and others who prefer to sit. Thus I have heard it sayd that if you and your mate enjoy each other whil'st hanging from a chandelier, it might be tryed, though it is fool-hardy and therefore not to be recommended.

A.E. Hall

A HAPPY ENDING

It is a common proverb amongst the men, that "Once a Whore and always a Whore." I have known this proverb crossed; and shall give you an account after what manner:

A country gentleman, who not having been in London in his life, or at least, not for a long time, being in conversation with some of his friends, heard them speak of the practice of lewd women, in picking men up in the streets. The gentleman could not believe any women could be so impudent, but he was resolved to make the experiment, and one evening in Fleet Street, he takes notice of a very pretty gentlewoman, which eyed him narrowly, whereupon he asked her to drink a glass of wine; she agreed at the first word and went with him to the next tavern.

He asked her how long she had continued that trade; she told him, as they all do, but a very short time. Then he continues, How can you dare to live in rebellion both against the laws of God and man, and destroy both your body and your immortal soul? She burst out into a flood of tears and told him it was pure necessity obliged her to it. Her father was a country gentleman who had extravagantly spent a plentiful estate, and left her unprovided for. She thought London was the best place to get her a livelihood in, and thither she came, but unfortunately fell into the hands of a lewd woman, who betrayed her to the lust of a gentleman, who was no more than once concerned with her, and then advised her to ply the streets; and that he himself was the first person that ever had picked her up.

The gentleman told her it was hard to believe persons could be guilty of such heinous crimes, and admonished her to forsake her evil practices. She gave him many thanks for his good advice. He told her, if she would resolve to amend for the future, he would take care to provide for her. They met again the next day, according to appointment, and he put her into a lodging he had provided, and being well assured of her repentance and sincerity, and finding her, moreover, an accomplished gentlewoman, soon after married her; and she made him a chaste and happy wife, and he lived as happily with her, as if she had been possessed of a portion of thousands of pounds.

PUT IT IN WRIGHTING

In Queene Elizabeth's time there lived in the cittie of London a merrie fellow named Hobson, a haberdasher dealer of small wares, dwelling at the lower end of Cheepside, in the Poultry. His Prentice, whom he had lately made a Freeman, came to him one day and sayd, "Sir, I have done your service long time fair and truly, now I pray you give me something to begin my fortune in the world." The Master sayd, "Ye speak well. Now I must shortly ride to Bristowe Fair and if you will bear my charges thither I will give you something that will be worth a hundred pounds." The servant accepted the commission and they set forth, till they came to their last lodging, when the servant sayd, "Now I have done as you commanded me and I pray you to tell me what I may have that will be worth a hundred pounds."

"Did I make this promise?"

"You did."

"Show it to me in wrighting."

"I have none."

"Then thou art like to have Nothing—and learn this—whensoever thou makest a bargain with any man, look thou take a wrighting for thy security, and be well advised how thou givest thy bond to another man; this thing has benefitted me in my time a hundred pounds, and so may it likewise do ye."

Mr. Hobson, having completed his businesse, he

had not ridden two miles on the road back to London but it began to raine, whereupon he called for his cloke of another servant that rode by, who sayd that it was left behind with the fellow that was with him: so they tooke shelter under a tree till he overtooke them. When he was come, Mr. Hobson sayd angrily: thou knave, where is my cloke that I left behind? Sir, and please you, answered the poore fellow, I have had to pawne it to pay for your charges all the way. Why knave, quoth Hobson, did'st not thou promise to bear my charges to Bristowe? Did I? sayd the fellow. Yes, you did, sayd Hobson. Shew me a wrighting then, the fellow answered. Whereunto Mr. Hobson answered little.

The Lyonne portrayed here has recently become the bride of a handsome (social) Lyon. She has been careful to guard her maine treasure (I speak not of her £300 a yeare) until the wedding bans were posted and the Bond set up in Wrighting. The other (who also loved the Lyon, not wisely, but too well) has onlie teares to shew for her over-generous nature and her unwise trust of a man's word, which is not always to be trusted. This storie may be of profitt to young ladies possessed of more Simplicitie than Sense.

GRUMBLINGS OF THE GIZZARD
OR
THE MYSTIC TWITCH

Here we have a young ladie in a pretty fix, for she hath two suitors. One is an old donkey of solidd substantial habits; the other a young Pudel (French dogge) who hath charm galore but not much besides. Now there is an old Proverb: "If thine enemy be in water up to the middle, lend him a hand to help him out; but if he stands up to the chin, set your Foot on his Head to thrust him in." One suitor must have a care that he do not bespatter and disparage his Rival unless he can be disposed of by some ingeniose method.

There is a sort of fellow who always doth Blabb that which proves Prejudicial to them; as those ridiculous Cod-Heads who are always saying: "I could never find a woman yet that lov'd me," whereas all the World knows that they are scarce good enough for the mannerly Dogs to hold up their Legs against and civilly to piss upon. Many, to render their Rivals odious, do usually draw them in such character, viz., "That Fellow is the happiest Fool in the World—For though he is not endowed with the Charms of Beauty, nor with the Gravity of Prudence—yet all the Women in the Country stick up their Tails and gad after him; and are at cuff and kick for the enjoyment of him." Such words do but assist your Rival, for Women are ever apt to favour the Unfortunate.

Ariel Hall

I am inclined to think that the Blessed Sex want Precepts concerning the Art of Love. That she may not miscarry in her Amours, nor become a Prey to the most Subtile Passion, Let her be sure to observe this General Rule, viz., "Not too easily Believe (more than is meet) that she is belov'd." Let her beware of thinking that any Man admires her because he discourses volubly of the Passion; and if he be immodest that talks with her, Let a Blush discover her Dislike of his Language. Young Ladies must always remember: "Men make greater Professions of Love than Women."

But must a Young Lady make no return of Kindness? Must she eccho back no Sighs, or Amorous Groans? Not one Courteous Pressure of Treading Toe? or Private Invitation of Mystic Twitch?

Now, by way of Reply to this, I say—if she smile on any, Let him enjoy that Sunshine of her Face to whom she intends to resign up her Dear Self. For, if she is too Prodigal of her Private Treads and Twinckles, of her Secret Squeezes and Mystic Twitches where No Marriage Noose is intended, her Petulant Forwardness creates a Suspicion of Unlawful Desires.

Another Caution to be observ'd: "Not to have too great a Conceit of their Handsomeness." This gives occasion to hop over and transgress the bounds of Modesty, and they fancy they are observ'd and lov'd for their bonny Carriage. But they are much deceiv'd: for if there be any mouths that water at them, or any Bellies that wamble after them, the Inclination proceeds in most instances from the Dishonest Hopes of enjoying them. I would not have mistresses take away all Hope, but only frustrate Dishonest Expectations. Men's Humours differ according to the variety of Female Tempers; some have such a veneration as that they dare not offer up an obsequious Amour nor presume to discompose the Gravity of her Bum with the Merry Touch of an extended Hop-Pole.

'Tis more convenient therefore rather by Signs and Proofs, rather than by Words and Letters to signify your Passion. So that we may safely affirm that the Eyes are the Authors and Dispensers of Love, especially if they retain a natural, majestick sweetness; or a pleasant Blackness, or a chearful caeruleousness, or lastly, have such piercing glances, which dive and enter into the very Recesses of the Soul. And thus you see, how by this way, a Lover may win his Desires and discover the Grumblings of his Gizzard to his dear Lady. But now, if these Betrayers of Love are not artificially manag'd, they will be apt to blabb, by an untoward Goggle, the Disorders and Perturbations of an enamour'd Soul. Let a Prudent Lover therefore tye up his looks and not suffer them to rove unseasonably. Is it not better to Bill in open view, and to toy it in Publick, than to smack it in the dark and to be jumbling in hugger-mugger behind the door? Gallants always keep the Love and Favour of their Mistresses by the same means they first obtain'd it: namely by pleasing them; by being obsequious to them; and by offering no occasion of offence.

(*Advice to Lovers,* by R. W. 1680)

AN OLD STORIE, WITH A NEW DEFINITION

Who does not remember the storie of Queen Elizabeth and Edward de Vere, Earl of Oxford? The Queen, residing that summer at Greenwich, was walking from the Presence chamber to the Royal Chapel, as was her wont on a Sunday morning. Her gown was of white silk embroidered with pearls the size of beans, overwhich was a black silk mantle shot with silver. Her wig was auburn and her eyes small, yet pleasant. Her teeth, when she smiled, were black. Great numbers of people waited for her procession—the Gentlemen, the Barons, the Earls, and the Knights of the Garter. The floor was strewn with rushes and the walls hung with fine tapestries. All kneeled as the Queen passed and to some she spoke a few words in a gentle voice and gave her hand to kiss. One of these was the Earl of Oxford. He made a low obeisance, but in doing so, had the misfortune to let a loud fart. This so distressed him that he left hurriedly and travelled abroad for seven years. On his return he went once again to Court. The queen welcomed him back and said most graciously: "My Lord, I had forgot the fart."

Some years later 'twas Sir John Suckling who wrote: "Love is the fart of everie heart; it paines a man when 'tis kept close, and other doth offend when 'tis let loose."

(*Sir John Suckling*, 1609-1641)

The HE - FLEA and the SHE - FLY had
not much in common.

THE CURE FOR A NAGGING WYFE

It has been wisely sayd that opposite ideas do not well on the same bolster. A He-Flea and a She-Fly had marryed contrary to the advyce of their Friends and Relations, for they consider'd they had not much in the way of Common-tastes. Yet it had been the onlie match available to them at the time; besides they were younge and impulsive. Flea had his habitts which pleas'd him and Fly likewise, the things that pleas'd her. Flea was very content to dwell in a bit of hay, or on the back of a dog (though 'twas true he sometimes lodg'd with respecktible gentlemen, as Samuel Pepys, who once counted twenty in his periwig) but he had little ambition to improve his estate. Fly, on the contrary, lov'd constant excitement and variety; she travell'd widely and enjoy'd seeing the world. In the way of victualls, too, she had much choyce and would often-times sup very daintily at the Queen's own table.

Now the She-Fly felt that her mate had onlie a certain Contrarinesse of Disposition else he could explore the world with her and enjoy the finer things of life. She harrass'd him daily with such words as: "You could fly if you would but try." "You could hum; You could sing; You could attract attention instead of always hiding in the remotest corner." Most importantly, she strove to impress upon this

Flea she had married that he must endeavour to associate with a better class of society. Flea answered nothing, but clung to his ways, which suited him very well; he paid no attention to the naggings and pesterings of his wyfe and spent many a night away from his bedd. When he consulted his friends as to how he might rid himself of this unhappy state he was told: "Only God and great sickness can cure a nagging wyfe."

THE DANGERS OF FLYING

The Philosophers of King Charles's reign were busy in finding out the Art of Flying. John Wilkins, Bishop of Chester,* has writ a book, dedicated to Lord Henry, Earl of Huntingdon, which affirms that the Moon may be a World; he doubts not but that in the next age it will be as usual to hear a man call for his wings, as it is now to call for his boots. He claims that a Journey to the Moon will be possible in the near future. Now the Wits of the age have made considerable sport of this passion of the good Bishop. One claims that he can already fly near as well as a turkey-cock, having practiced considerably, by hop, step and jump in his rooms. He promises on the next Thanksgiving Day, to fly over Fleet-Street and to light on the May-Pole in the Strand.

A critick of this nefarious notion, who writes for the *Guardian*, is resolved to prevent these ideas from taking root. Why, said he, it will fill the World with Innumerable Immoralties. Young lovers could make a midnight assignation on the Cupola of St. Pauls', so that it would ressemble nothing so much as a pigeon-house when covered with young coxcombs and wenches. A desperate young blade might be able to fly in a Lady's window during the darkest hours

*Bishop Wilkins wrote *The Discovery of a New World*; or a Discourse "tending to prove that it is probable there may be another World in the Moon; with a Discourse concerning the Possibility of a Passage thither, 1638."

and the husband, sleeping below, would be never the wiser. He might, indeed, clip his wife's wings, but what would that avail, with flocks of Whore-Masters hovering perpetually over the house? One could never be sure of the morality of the female members of the family; the expense alone would be horrendous for the hiring of a wing'd Chaperone.

No doubt, by means of wings, much more could be accomplished in much less time; but of what benefit would that be to the Public Morals? This iniquitous Invention must not be encourag'd.

THE IMPORTANCE OF FLEEING

A young lad of seventeen has been recently brought to trial for robbing a servant-maid of her pockets in St. Paul's churchyard. The evidence of the maid is given, as follows:

And please you, my Lord, I had been at Drury Lane play-house to see, *The Country Wife*—a baddish sort of play it turned out. So, walking home, all alone by myself through St. Paul's church-yard, this young man overtook me, and would needs have a kiss of me. Oho! young spark, thought I to myself,—we have all been to the play—but if a kiss will content you, why, e'en take it, and go about your business; for you shall have nothing more from me, I promise you. This I said to myself, my Lord, while the young man was kissing me. But, my Lord, he went on to be quite audacious; so I stood still against a tree, without so much as speaking a word; for I had a mind to see how far his impudence would carry him. But—all at once, when I was thinking of no such thing, C-R-A-C-K went my pocket-strings, and away ran the young man with the pockets in his hand. And then I thought it was high time to cry out: so I roared: "Murder" and "Stop Thief" till the watchman took hold of him and carried us both before the constable. And please you, my Lord, I was never in such a flurry in my life; for who would have thought of any such things from so good-looking a young man?

OF CORPULENCY, DYET, AND THE HIGH COST OF LIVING

It is generally agreed that there is sublimity in vastness; therefore it must be concluded that corpulent people fill a large space in society and are great objects of interest. The Ancients considered the stomach to be the seat of our noblest faculties and affections, of pride and courage. Persians called it the dispenser of genius; Hebrews considered it the seat of intellect; Hindoos reverence it as the source of thought. Shakespeare knew its importance; Fontenelle declared that there was no enjoying life without a good one—"to enjoy life, it is necessary to have a bad heart and a good stomach."

Corpulence is often attractive to the fair sex, as giving importance to a suitor; and not only this, there are the double advantages of a comfortable resting place and the merry spirit which often accompanies those whose figures are well upholstered. A Peacock of large girth, portrayed here with his mate, appears the very picture of contentment. His wife stuffs him well and even takes care to slip a lump of butter and a glass of brandy into his gruel—but unfortunately he died recently, suffocated by his own fat. Now his disconsolate widow is in fine feather for another. This is not the first instance of a worthy person kindly coddled out of the world.

The majority of those who suffer the disease of corpulence would seek a specific or pill to tame the appetite. I am acquainted with but one. Avicenna gives a receipt for some pills to be taken as a preservative against hunger, which is as follows:

"Take of sweet almonds one pound; the like quantity of beef-suet; of oil of violets two ounces; a sufficient quantity of mucilage; and of the roots of marsh-mallows, one ounce; let altogether be brayed in a mortar, and made into bolusses about the bigness of a common nut. It is of the utmost consequence in the cure of Obesity to take off the pinguifying propensities of the appetite." Of this Avicenna seems to have been aware, and he recommends those who cannot swallow the pills, to take the remedy in a fluid state, i.e., "one pound of oil of violets mixed with melted beef-suet. A person taking this may fast for ten days without the least hunger!!"

Doubtless this would answer the purpose full as well as a certain French alimentary powder, Raleigh's tobacco or the German girdle. The Mistress of Arden has advocated a sudorific system, of hot sand baths, stoves and stews; but one man who feared the effects of over-stewing said he had all the ingredients at home—with a large fire, a very fat wife, and a son who kept him in a perpetual fever.

Good health is a jewel necessary to both life and love. A doctor may assist you, but those who practice the qualities of self-denial, hard work, exercise and cheerfulness will need no diet-drinks, boxes of pills, nor gally-pots.

"Laugh and grow fat" is an old adage; we are told that every time a man laughs, he adds something to his life. Dr. Sydenham said that the arrival of a merry-andrew in a town was more beneficial to the lives of its inhabitants than twenty asses loaded with medecine. Mr. George Jones seems to have had this object in view in his "Friendly Pills" which were to make patients of all complexions laugh at the time of taking them, and to cure all curable complaints. "Pills to Purge the Paines of Love" has much the same object, since laughter and love are a marvellous combination. People who can laugh together can live happily together.

It is entirely possible to live and be healthy on very little food. Mr. Crabb, an ornamental hermit, allowed himself but three farthings a week to live on. Another man lived on a pint of tea daily, chewing, but not swallowing, a few raisins and almonds. An old Turk ate daily four ounces of rice, thirty cups of coffee, three drachms of opium and sixty pipes of tobacco. But it is not wise to give up eating entirely. One lady nearly lost her life through the notion that no fat person could get to Heaven, and one Quaker refused to eat because he read that man shall not live by bread alone, but by the Word of God. He did not survive.

In the present time of "high prices" particularly of meat, I like to remember an old friend who said that in his forefathers' time pudding was set first on the table; thereby diminishing the desire for meat, and halving the food bills, not to mention Bills of Mortality (for the quantity of animal food thrown into the stomach without sufficient mastication is the great cause of most disease.)

Doctors, hairdressers and house-maids being also at a premium nowadays; not to mention the Churches ever needing funds, and Drugs so dear, I have been requested to insert this advertisement on behalf of a family who wish to consolidate the expenses of their bodies and souls:

Wanted for a family, who have bad health, a sober steady person, in the capacity of Doctor, Surgeon, Apothecary and Man-midwife. He must occasionally act as butler, and dress hair and wigs. He will be required sometimes to read prayers, and to preach a sermon every Sunday. A good salary will be given.

(*enquire of Abel Drugger, at the little North doore of S. Paule's Church, signe of The Gunne.*)

LOOSE DAMES

If for thyself thou wilt not watch thy whore,
Watch her for me, that I may love her more,
What comes with ease we nauseously receive,
Who, but a sot, would scorn to love with leave?

With hopes and fears my flames are blown up higher?
Make me despair, and then I can desire.
Give me a jilt to teaze my jealous mind;
Deceits are virtues in the female kind.

Corinna my fantastic humour knew,
Play'd trick for trick, and kept herself still new:
She, that next night I might the sharper come,
Fell out with me, and sent me fasting home;

Or some pretence to lie alone would take;
Whene'er she pleas'd, her head and teeth would ake;
'Till having won me to the highest strain,
She took occasion to be sweet again.

With what a gust, ye gods, we then embrac'd!
How every kiss was dearer than the last!
Thou whom I now adore, be edify'd,
Take care that I may often be deny'd.

Forget the promis'd hour, or feign some fright,
Make me lie rough on bulks each other night.
These are the arts that best secure thy reign,
And this the food, that must my fires maintain.

Loose dames are but flatter'd, never lov'd.

Gross easy love does, like gross diet, pall,
In squeasy stomachs honey turns to gall.
Had Danae not been kept in brazen tow'rs,
Jove had not thought her worth his golden show'rs,

When Juno to a cow turn'd Io's shape
The watchman help'd her to a second leap.
Let him who loves an easy Whetstone whore
Pluck leaves from trees, and drink the common store.

The jilting harlot strikes the surest blow,
A truth which I by sad experience know.
The kind poor constant creature we despise;
Man but pursues the quarry while it flies.

(Ovid's *Amours*, Book II Eleg. 19,
trans. by John Dryden)

REFLEXIONS ON LOVE

I have been furnished with severall Maxims on Love by a gentleman of experience, who assures me they are the result of long and profound reflection, and that they deserve to be brought to the attention of the public:

"There are more calamities in the world arising from love than from hatred."

"Love is the daughter of Idleness, but the Mother of Disquietude."

"The gay part of Mankind is most amorous, the serious, most loving."

"A Coquette often loses her reputation while she preserves her virtue."

"A Prude often preserves her reputation when she has lost her virtue."

"Love refines a man's behaviour, but makes a woman's ridiculous."

"The endeavours to revive a decaying passion generally extinguish the remains of it."

Love has been known to cause despair even in men of the highest intelligence. John Milton, our great poet, once cried: "Oh! Why did God create this novelty on earth—this fair defect of nature? and not fill the world at once with men, as angels, without feminine!"

MISS FANNY FICKLE AND MR. NORMAN KNOW-ALL

Miss Fanny Fickle and Mr. Norman Know-All was about to get married and on the way to the altar—nay on the very steps of the church, Miss Fickle sayd: "I must tell you that I shall only marrie you on certain Conditions."

What are those, pray tell? asked Mr. Know-All.

I shall lay alone in my bed, sayd she.

If you lay alone, I shall not, he replied.

I shall eat alone, she sayd.

Well then, I shall eat at the club, was his answer.

And I shall be angrie without occasion, she continued.

Never fear, I shall give you plentie of occasion, was his answer.

As for Sex, she sayd, I believe its pleasure is highly over-estimated.

That may be trew, he sayd, but a thing must not be condemned before it is sampled.

Furthermore, was her last remark before stepping up to the Altar, the Position is ridiculous!

I'll make thee a Wager on that, whispered Mr. Know-All . . . !

The only objection that Miss Fickle seems to insinuate against the gentleman is his want of complaisance, which, I perceive, she is very willing to return. Now I can discover from this very circum-

Ariel Hall

stance, that she and her lover, whatever they may think of it, are very good friends in their hearts. It is difficult to determine whether love delights more in giving pleasure or pain. Let Miss Fickle ask her own heart, if she doth not take a secret pride in making this man of good sense look very silly. Hath she ever been better pleased than when her behaviour hath made her lover ready to hang himself? It is not impossible that her lover may have discovered her tricks, and hath a mind to give her as good as she sends. I remember a handsome young woman who treated a gentleman just come down from Oxford, as if he had been a barbarian. The first week after she had fix'd him, she took a pinch of snuff out of his rival's box, and wilfully touch'd the enemy's little finger. She scarce ever wrote a letter to him without mispelling his name. She made an assignation with him fourscore miles from London; but, as he was very well acquainted with her pranks, he took a journey quite the contrary way. Accordingly they met, quarreled, and in a few days were married. Their former hostilities are now the subject of their mirth, being at present content with that part of love only which bestows pleasure.

Besides, Miss Fickle may consider that, as there are often faults concealed before marriage, so there are sometimes many virtues unobserv'd. Women who have been married some time, not having it in their heads to draw after them a numerous train of followers, find their satisfaction in the possession of one man's heart. It is true that some ladies in their bloom desire to be excused in this particular. But, when time hath worn out their natural vanity and taught them discretion, their fondness settles on its proper object. And it is probably for this reason, that among husbands, you will find more that are fond of women beyond their prime than of those who are actually in the insolence of beauty. My reader will apply the same observation to the opposite sex.

"I cannot choose but kisse thee with my lippes..."

THE KISSE

The more I do behold thy face, the more my mind
  doth vaunt.
This face is of favour, those cheeks are reddy and
  white;
Those lips are cherry red, and full of deepe delight.
Quick rowling eyes, the temples high, and forehead
  white as snow;
The eye-brows seemely set in frame, with dimpled
  chin below.
O! how beautie hath adorned thee with every seemely
  hew.
In limbs, in looks, with all the rest proportion keeping
  dew.
Sure, I have not seene a finer soule in every kinde of
  part:
I cannot choose but kisse thee with my lippes, and
  love thee with my heart.

(from *The Three Ladies of London,* 1584)

THE DISADVANTAGES OF EXCESSIVE HOUSE-CLEANING

A gentleman of my acquaintance is married to a lady of agreable disposition, who is much praised by all the good women of her parish as being the neatest house-keeper they ever knew. My friend finds this extraordinary neatness so troublesome that he claims he would rather lodge in a carriers' Inn or take up his abode with the horses in the stable.

He does not object to a moderate amount of cleanliness and neatness; yet he does not wish to wash his hands six times a day, like the superstitious Mahometans nor does he enjoy having his house rendered useless to him by the continual house-cleaning that his wife and her servant seem to judge necessary. He says that he cannot see the difference between having a house that is always dirty and one that is always to be cleaned. He is disturbed all the day long by the noise of beating the carpets, scrubbing the floors, washing the windows and airing the rooms. He must go from room to room while the one is to be dusted, the other dry-rubbed, another to be run over with a dry-mop and so on.

Not a speck of dirt is ever allowed to rest on the floor. All who come to the house are obliged to rub their shoes for half an hour on a large mat at the entrance; after which they must hop, skip and jump from one mat to another, ranged at certain distances from each other in the passage, and so they enter a room, exhausted from their efforts.

This extraordinary solicitude of his wife for the care and preservation of her house and her furnishings makes his house quite useless to him, and takes away all the ease and comfort which is the chief pleasure of a home.

This superabundant neatness was also the means of his losing a very considerable addition to the family fortune.

A rich old uncle came up to town last summer on purpose to pay my friend and his wife a visit. After supper the old gentleman desired to have his pipe; but this could by no means be allowed lest the stench of the tobacco could never be got out of the furniture. The old uncle had brought a favorite pointer with him, who, at his first coming, was immediately locked up in the coal-bin. But the dog found means to escape; crept slyly upstairs and stretched himself out on a fine damask settee. The wife treated the animal to a taste of the whip and when the uncle objected, it produced such high words between them, that he called for his horse and swore he would never darken the doors of my friend's house again. He went home and about two months after, he died; but as he could not forgive the ill treatment which both he and his dog had received, he had altered his will, which, before, had been made out entirely in my friend's favour.

"... Another man's dishe may be as goode as my owne."

THE COOKE AND THE WENCH

A Man that was a Cooke maried a countrie Wench that some time before had the Mischance to lose her Maydenhead to another. When they came to lay together on their Wedding Night, he putt his hand on her bellie and was mightily surprized to finde a monstrous commotion therein. What, Wyfe! sayd he, is there already Fleshe in thy Pott? Aye, sayd she,—and that's why I maried a Cooke. He happen'd to be of an extreamlie goode Nature and so he sayd, Well,—I'll not make a greatt Stewe about it. Another Man's Dishe may be as goode as my owne. So, they liv'd harmoniously together and the Cooke has the Benefitt of a contented Wyfe (who has thenceforth mended her Ways) as well as a fine Broth of a Sonne by another Man's Laboure.

Provide for thy husband to make him good cheer
Make merry together what time ye be here
A-Bed and at Board, howsoever befall
Whatever God sendeth, be Merry withall.

A NEW PERSPECTIVE

This picture is upside-down, you cry, (and wish to blame the printer!)—but it is done with a high purpose,: namely, to disturb the rigid conceptions of some otherwise worthy intellects. To turn things upside-down is not always successful, as was seen recently in the case of Thomas Hobsil, who desired to be rid of some two hundred small pebbles he had swallowed to cure his windiness. The Dr.'s treatment was to hang him upside-down, bound to a ladder, but the pebbles were heard to fall back in place when he righted himself. Nor do we know the eventual fate of a distinguished military man who desired to be buried head down, for he wrote in his will: "Since the world is now topsy-turvy, I expect eventually to be right side up." Painters have a trick of turning their canvasses upside-down to tell if all is in balance. I suggest that it might be a good practice for a man to occasionally turn the canvas of his life upside-down: something on the order of a Spring house-cleaning. He might throw aside useless baggage, or re-arrange the furnishings, or decide to put in new ones. He may thus find things worth keeping and things to throw away, or even find in long-forgotten seeds of thought, some new idea. Stagnation of thought is death; the struggle between good and evil is necessary to life; to hold hardened ideas of these is to calcify that which should be fluid.

An ancient story may further clarify my thoughts on this subject, particularly for those aggravated members of the fair sex whose mates are sometimes enticed into promiscuity.

A Bishop, riding a mare on his way to the Cathedral, was forced to halt whilst the mare accepted the attentions of a stallion. The stallion had left his mate in a near-by field to accomplish the mission, and returned to her afterwards, quickly forgetting the whole business. So, I suggest that adultery must not always be considered grounds for divorce, nor should sex be confused with love. Sex and love are two different things: the one being physical and the other spiritual, a different view might be beneficial to those whose attitudes have become hardened with intolerant thinking. A general cleansing of the cerebral dust and clutter is recommended at least twice each year. When you are rid of out-worn prejudice you may be in a place where love is not far distant; at least this was the opinion of a worthy philosopher.

THE SALUTARY EFFECT OF MUSIC

Connubial miseries are not uncommon in youth as well as in the middle years when the vital powers are declining. Dr. Samuel Johnson has remarked, with what I consider some injustice, that those who suffer thus are as happy as their natures would allow in any other circumstances. I have the temerity to take issue with him, and to venture a new medecine for those who suffer in the bonds of an infelicitous marriage. What is this medecine? It is Music.

How feeble is our knowledge, and how mysterious and inscrutable are the ways of Nature. Music alone, with the aid of Nature, has cured the deadly bite of a tarantula; Sciatica has been removed with Song; Deafness destroyed by the sound of a trumpet. An eminent composer of my acquaintance once fell ill of a fever and believing his end near, requested to hear some music in his room, though 'twas against the advice of his physician. In ten days, by the continuance of the music, he grew entirely well, without any other remedies but two bleedings in the foot, followed by a strong purge. Indeed, every malady has, at some time or other, yielded to the power of melody. Why then, should not an unhappy marriage?

A celebrated physician says that musical vibrations soothe the nerves which communicate with the brain, thus expelling the poisons and procuring harmony and health. He advises that the wise will choose their music well, as certain exaggerated sounds, mistakenly called "Music" by our present generation, can also cause pain, excitability and distress.

A PETITION OF THE LADIES OF LONDON AND WESTMINSTER

TO THE HONOURABLE HOUSE FOR HUSBANDS,

PRINTED IN LONDON, FOR

MARY WANTMAN

Sirs: We have been treated with much unfairness by the gentlemen of this city. The holy state of Matrimony has been scorned at court; persecuted in sonnet by the Poets, and ridiculed in the play-house. Batchelors have expressed fear lest they suffer from headache within two weeks of marriage and that a wife is likely to reduce them to mere skin and bones. Others persist they have an incurable aversion to squalling children, midwives, nurses, coddles, pins, etc. etc. They all express fear the taxes will run high.

We petition first: that all men should be obliged to marry as soon as they are one and twenty, and that those who refuse to obey this law shall be required to pay tax to the King for the expence of his army in Flanders. Second: that no excuse shall be admitted, save only frigidity or impotence, which shall be adjudicated by a Board of Matrons. Third: that since Wine is the chiefest enemy of Marriage, none but men who are already married may enter a Tavern. Lastly: that the propagation of mankind should be considered of more importance than the draining of Fens and the converting of Pasture-Land, whilst so many Ladies are left unploughed, unharrowed and uncultivated.

"... Rich widows are besieged e'er their first husbands are cold."

To this has been subsequently printed (in 1693) a

PETITION OF THE WIDOWS, by the WIDE-O'S. Widows claim to know a man's value too well, not to regret the loss of so serviceable a creature. We all had good husbands, they say, and, though we had reason to complain of them when alive, we now forgive them for leaving us once more to ourselves. There are, so we are told, four classes of widows: Old Widows, Rich Widows, Young Widows and Poor Widows. Old Widows claim to be the best for keeping a young man warm in bed. Rich widows have no problem, since they are besieged on all sides e'er their first husbands are cold. Young widows are the most numerous, especially since the Wars have made so much Havock among the husbands. It is pretended, by some of finicky taste, that widows lack a Maiden-head, but we see no reason why a young widow may not be as capable of obliging these criticks as the Best Virgin in the world. It is by using a few astringents before, and at the critical minute, crying out, "Fie Sir,—Pray Sir,—will you split me up? Will you murder me alive?" Indeed, we promise them to howl, sigh, and roar as heartily as an ox when he's led to the slaughter house.

A late Monarch, who was inferior to none but Solomon, was often heard to say that the getting of a Maiden-head was a drudgery fit for none but Porters. To conclude: a Widow is a Tried Gun and carries the Tower-Mark upon her; now who knows but a Maid may split in the proving?

The Batchelors have responded to these Petitions with one of their own; but, as their case is very weak, it will not be printed here, for it is not worth the Printer's ink.

(*Harleian Miscellanies*—Vol X)

ON CHUSING A WYFE

It is not always to the advantage of a Commonwealth to be overstocked with Beauties. They are undoubtedly the most suitable furniture for Public Places—but it is beleeved by some that your plain woman, whose understanding is not perverted by Admiration, often makes the discreetest and best Mother and companyon.

You will remember that King Henry the 8th had six wives; the first, he divorced; the head of the second (beautiful Anne Boleyn) was surgically removed; whilst the third died in childbirth. After her death it was necessary to search for a fourth but not everyone was anxious for the honour. Holbein, the court-painter, was sent to draw the portrait of Christiana, Dowager Duchess of Milan. She refused Henry's offer of matrimony, however, and wrote: "I have but one head; had I two, one of them should be at Your Majesty's service."

So the search continued. Holbein was next sent to Flanders to draw the head of Lady Anne of Cleve; making so favourable a likeness that marriage was agreed on. But when Lady Anne arrived in England the King was monstrously disappointed. "You would have me wed this Flanders mare?" he roared at Cromwell, his Chancellor of State. "I will have your head for this!" Diplomacy demanded that the marriage take place, but it was quickly annulled; Anne was grateful

The advantages of a Plain Woman

to be allowed to keep her head and to remain in England as a "Sister." She behaved discreetly and always showed great kindness to Henry's children.

The Camel and the Elephant we see here are about to part before the wedding ceremony. The elephant sayd that a Camel was doubtless interesting to look at but that he would not be married to one. What a Pittie! 'Tis sayd that an Elephant never forgets, but methinks this one forgot that a Plain Woman often becomes beautiful through Love and Marriage. Wherein, then, doth Beauty lie?

THE SHE-WEDDING
OR
A MAD MARRIAGE
BETWEEN MARY, A SEAMAN'S MISTRESS
AND
MARGARET, A CARPENTER'S WIFE
AT DEPTFORD

It hath been the policy of the prince of darkness in all ages, when any work of his was to be carried on, which required a more than ordinary cunning, to employ a female craft therein: a remarkable instance whereof I shall here present you with.

At Deptford in the county of Kent, at the sign of the King's Head, for some time past, as a maid-servant in the house, there hath lived one Mary, who pretended herself, in her conversation, reserved and honest enough for one of her age, being thirty or thereabouts, till about seven or eight months past she used to keep company with one Charles Parsons, a young man lately gone to sea, with whom she was observed to be somewhat familiar; insomuch that the neighbors looked upon her as either married to him, or at least as free of her favours as if she had; her mistress began to suspect that her sweetheart had given her a belly full of love, as afterwards it proved to be true. This Mary did admit that Charles Parsons was the father of her unborn babe, being about six months gone, and applied herself to his mother, saying that they were married and desiring her to assist her to her lying-down.

The old mother doubted thereof and urged that she produce her certificate and that if she found the same true, she would provide for her.

This answer put to Mary caused her to set her wits to the rack how she should deceive the mother; wit being the strongest when necessity is the strongest, she was resolved to advise with a neighbor of hers that was her friend, and by name Margaret, the wife of a carpenter living hard by. This Margaret remembered the story of two men, that had a design on a parson's wife, agreed to dress the youngest in women's cloaths, and accordingly to marry each other; thereby designing, by a liberal reward to the parson, to spend their first night in the parson's house and play the love-scuffle. By which opportunity, whilst the parson was at his morning studies, the party that was enamoured of the good man's wife changed beds to enjoy the real wife; which design, the parson not at all suspecting, readily assented to and ignorantly brought cuckolddom upon himself. Remembering this story, as I say, the ladies consented with themselves, that two women might as well commit matrimony as two men.

The carpenter's wife gets a suit of her husband's cloaths, in which she arrays herself, and sets to work (without her chief tool) to act the man's part; and away they trudged for St. George's Church in Southwark. The minister and the clark consented unto, but in the time of administering the ceremony they began to hesitate at what they were a-doing and that she was not what she represented. When she was to answer those words, I Charles take thee Mary &c. she mistook the words, and cried, I Margaret; but she excused it and carried on the deceit. The ceremony being ended, Margaret took the clark aside and told him that he had dabbled with his wife before marriage and had got her with child, being near six months, and desired that the certificate might be antedated; which for a reward he consented to. They departed for Deptford and produced the certificate for the old Mrs. Parsons, with her son's name duly written and the false date.

But so it is that most of the sex are apt to brag of their intrigues, and most especially when they are together toping their noses over the brandy bottle, or hot suppings, this intrigue came to a discovery. Several of the neighbors talked of the change in Mary's condition, but Mary and Margaret lovingly called each other by the name of husband and wife, saying they knew a couple six weeks wedded with not one bout since they were married.

"Not one bout?" replied an old woman,—" I would cut off the tool of that husband that should have a wife for two days and nights and never put it to the exercise that God made it for."

"Some Rogue!" replies another, "to tantalise a wife after that rate."

"Did I know the dull dog," pursues a third, "I would set him up for all our neighbors in Deptford and Greenwich, to make a public pissing-post of!"

"Intolerable," says a fourth,—"If I pawned my

petticoat that covered me, I would have some honest fellow to relieve me, and make him do it before the Rogue's face."

Some of this discourse being related to the old Mother Parsons, she resolved to go and inquire at the church where the certificate had been issued, and no such persons were found to have been married at the date mentioned, which had been predated by six months, as you will recall. Home goes the old woman, and discards her supposed daughter from her favour; declaring to all the neighbors how base a trick had been put upon her. Insomuch that it became the publick discourse of the whole town,—the young maids laughing at the flat sport they had the first night; the graver matrons, at the impudence of the parties that should so disgrace the state of matrimony. The parson that married them, made a complaint to the civil magistrate, who committed them both to the Round-House in Greenwich, where Margaret hath since been bailed out, and Mary yet continues there.

SINGLE BLESSEDNESS

To a friend who wrote that he wished he had never married and desired advice as to how he might escape his unfortunate situation, Bishop Redfield answered: "You don't know the art of getting quit of a wife? This is how to do it:—Never, NEVER contradict her; this will deprive her of an exercise most healthful to women. But, Odzooks, contradict her—you open the floodgates; you provide the greatest tonic to her lungs and circulation. Contradiction and Quarrel are *optima medicamente* for all members of the female tribe."

And Aesop tells the story of a Lyon so enamoured of a young lady that he consented to her Father's request that his teeth be drawn and his nails pared. He presented himself at her door in this condition; but the Father had been the sharper of the two; for the Lyon having thus been rendered helpless was met with a club and advised never to darken the door again.

Then there was my friend, Mr. W. H., who claim'd to know as much of the female world as any man in Great Britain—though truth to tell, he owned that the chiefest part of his knowledge was "That they are NOT TO BE KNOWN."

He had laid siege to several heiresses successively. With the first he seemed to be on the verge of success —but alas, she ran off one night with the family

WELCOME

butler. Next he tried a wealthy widow; she cool'd his ardour when she suggested that he show his bank account to her lawyer. The third lady confided to her maid that she had seldom seen so fine a pair of spindle-shanks as Mr. H. possessed; yet, for some unaccountable reason she would not have him. The fourth was an elderly lady of considerable property whom he thinks he came close to capturing. The news of this imminent danger was conveyed by gossip and by post to her relations. They came pouring in from all parts of England. "My dear—how could you—?" "—" "most unsuitable"—"what a frightful mistake—" "How fortunate we've come—" —"the last person in the world—" Still Mr. H. was of the opinion that he might have become a married man had not she been carried off by a hard frost.

Then there was the bachelor who married late in life, hoping to spend his declining years in peace and quiet. He married a Good Woman—which, according to some Ale-House signs is a woman without a head. The principal virtue of a woman (so he wrote me) should be Silence. His wife promptly hung up a parrot in the parlour; she never failed to interrupt his speeches; she always finished his conversations and stories by telling them louder than he could. She chose a house next a church where there was perpetual bell-ringing every hour of the day and night. Certain young people of the parish also delighted in what is call'd "Rough Music"—consisting of performances on Cow-Horns, Salt-Boxes, Warming-Pans, Wash-Tubs, etc. With so much noise in the daytime, he frequently dream'd of it at night, and at last was convinc'd that there could be no peace for him but in the Grave.

Good Queen Bess enjoy'd Single Blessedness, and was put much out of Humour when any persons of her Court desired to take a mate. When she ask'd the Ladies of her Chamber if they lov'd to think of Matrimony, those who were wise conceal'd their opinion. 'Twas said that for a Courtier to be in favour with the Queen, he must be out of favour with his wife. A Courtier who married without her consent was apt to spend his honeymoon in the Tower. (This happened to Sir Walter Raleigh). A young lady-in-waiting once had the misfortune to admit to the Queen that she had indeed thought much about Matrimonie, but that she had been unable to get her Father's consent. "Indeed?" replied the Queen, "Then I will sue for you to your Father." She was as good as her word. The young ladie was call'd in, and told that her Father had given his consent. "Thank you, Your Majestie," she ventur'd timidly—"I will be very happy, and please Your Majestie." "So thou shalt," said Elizabeth, "but not to be a Fool, and Marry! Your Father's consent was given to ME, and I shall keep it in my possession. Go to thy Businesse—thou art a Bold One."

CRUMMS FROM KING JAMES' TABLE

"A verie wise woman is a verie foolish thing."

* * * *

"A verie wise man and a verie fool do little harm; it is the mediocrity of wisdom that troubleth all the world."

WATCH OUT!!

for . . .

THE MONTH OF MAY

The MONTH of MAY is fraught with danger for the fair sex. As the poet tells us: "Flushed by the spirit of the genial year, be greatly cautious of your SLIDING HEARTS." A French countess has told me that although she could promise to be chaste in every month besides, she could not engage for herself in May. This admonition applies also to the Anglo-Saxon race, for May is a time of year which infuses a kindly warmth in all the earth and affects all of its inhabitants.

What is the cause of this recurring inclination? Is it that the Spirits having been, as it were, frozen and congealed all winter are now loosed and set a-rambling? Is it the pretty prospects of happy birds in every tree? Is it the sight of butterflies kissing the flowers? Of cocks chasing young chickens? Of stallions mounting mares? It is at this time that we see the young country wenches in a church parish dancing 'round a May pole, which one of our learned antiquaries supposes to be a relic of a certain pagan worship that I do not think proper to mention.

The same anniversary love-fit spreads through the whole sex, as Mr. Dryden well observes in his description of this merry month.

For thee, sweet month, the groves green liv'ries wear.
If not the first, the fairest of the year;
For thee the Graces lead the dancing hours,
And Nature's ready pencil paints the flow'rs.

The sprightly May commands our youth to keep
The vigils of her night, and breaks their sleep;
Each gentle breast with kindly warmth she moves,
Inspires new flames, revives extinguished loves.

Having thus fairly admonished the female sex, and laid before them the dangers they are exposed to in this critical month, I shall in the next place lay down some rules and directions for their better avoiding those calentures which are so very frequent in this season:—

In the first place, I would advise them never to venture abroad in the fields, but in the company of a parent, a guardian, or some other discreet person. I have before shewn how apt they are to trip in the flowery meadow; and shall further observe to them, that Prosperine was out a-maying when she met with that fatal adventure Milton describes when he mentions—

. . . that fair field
Of Enna, where Prosperine gathering flowers
Herself a fairer flower—was gather'd . . .

Since I am going into quotations, I shall conclude this head with Virgil's advice to young people, while they are gathering wild strawberries and nosegays that they should have a care of the "snake in the grass."

In the second place, I cannot but approve those prescriptions which our astrological physicians give in their almanacks for this month: such as "a spare and simple diet, with a moderate use of phlebotomy."

As I have often declared that I have nothing more at heart than the honour of my dear country-women,

I would beg them to consider, whenever their resolutions begin to fail them, that there are but one and thirty days of this soft season, and that if they can but weather out this one month, the rest of the year will be easy to them. As for that part of the fair sex who stay in town, I would advise them to be particularly cautious how they give themselves up to their most innocent entertainments. If they cannot forbear the playhouse, I would recommend tragedy to them rather than comedy; and should think the puppet show much safer than the opera, all the while the Sun is in Gemini.

The reader will observe, that this paper is written for the use of those ladies who think it worthwhile to war against nature in the cause of honour. As for that abandoned crew, who do not think virtue worth contending for, but give up their reputation at the first summons, such warnings and premonitions are thrown away upon them. A prostitute is the same easy creature in all the months of the year, and makes no difference between May and December.

THE BROAKEN HEART

A Doctor is often call'd as a last resort; it being generally thought that the treatment is more dangerous than the disease. We are fortunate in London to possess a most unorthodox physician, one Dr. Procter, who has had considerable success with his ingeniose remedies which display more common-sense than chemistry. He has no great liking for the gentry, however; will visit only when he so desires, and prescribe only when forc'd by untoward circumstance. A French Ambassador once paid him a visit, bowing several times verie low; but during this exercise, the Dr. flung his leg over the Frenchman's head, and went back to his studies. On another occasion a serving-man brought his master's water for the Dr. to look at; the Dr., refusing, the servant threw it in the Dr.'s face. This so pleas'd the Dr. that he saw the gent. and cur'd him.

He was once call'd to visit a young ladie who had rooms at the Savoy, on the water side. She complain'd of a broaken heart and said she was dyeing of it. The good Dr. sat by her bed but soon discover'd she was past the power of reason. Accordingly he plac'd her in a chair by the balcony; then, calling his two serving men, he directed that they heave her into the river. The surprize has absolutely cured her of her broaken heart, and she has never since complained of it.

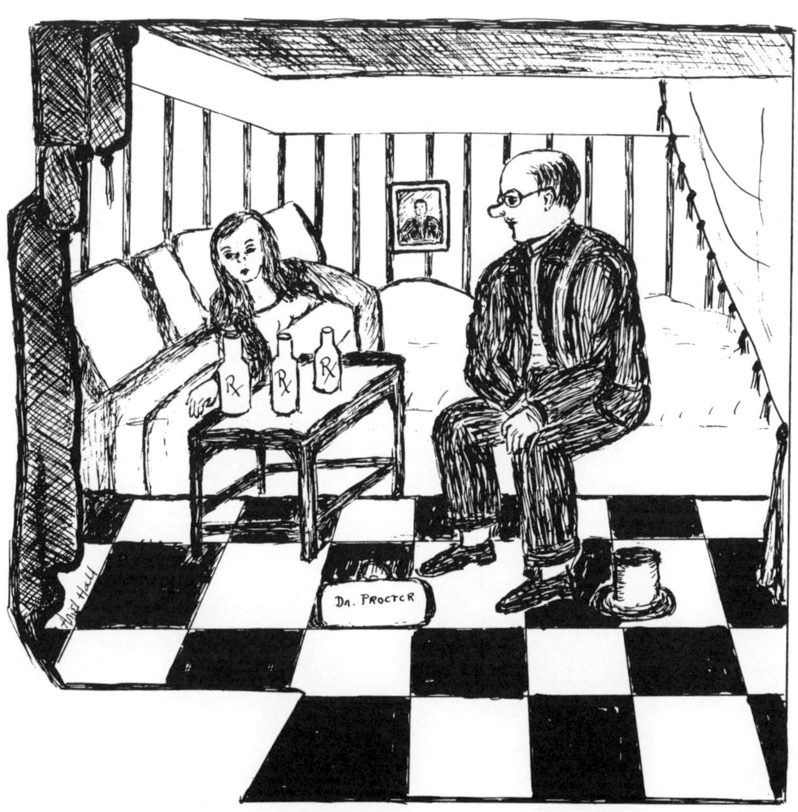

Oh, terrible tormentes . . .
Love is a parlous matter! How it runnes out of my nose!
It's now in my back, now in my belly, now in the bottom of my hose!

One day, as he was riding a strange horse to see a gent. who lay a-dyeing, the good Dr. dozed off; the animal, being thirsty, ducked his head into a pond, at which the Dr. slid over his neck and into the water; so he has had a taste of his own medecine. But, I forgott,—this story is about a broaken heart. It is difficult to cure, and few men are worth it.

LOVE IN A HOLLOW TREE
(A PLAY)

Approaching the conclusion of this book of PILLS, I cannot but recommend to your perusal a most exquisite comedy call'd LOVE in a Hollow Tree, (author anon.). It concerns both Love and Cookery. There are severall characters and many scenes which I shall condense for your convenience. The cast is as follows:

Favourite, the House-Keeper, who attends the wants of

Lady Bonona, who is the Mother of

Valentine, a very handsome young man.

Let-Acre, the Farmer

Mrs. Furiosa, a Widow, who has a daughter named

Florida, a beautiful young lady.

The play opens at the house of Lady Bonona with a scene of Good-Housewifry where Favourite makes this complaint to her mistress:

Fav.: The last mutton killed was lean, Madam. Should not some fat sheep be brought in?

Lady B.: What say you, Let-Acre, to it?

Let.: This is the worst time of year for sheep. The fresh grass makes them fall away, and they begin to taste of the wool. They must be spared for a while. I hope we shall have some fresh calves shortly.

This and other lively dialogue leads to the Second Act, in which *Valentine,* having in the First Act lost his way, while out hawking, sees a light in the distance and comes to the house of the *Widow Furiosa.* Her daughter *Florida* is working on a parchment and the maid is spinning. Sack is call'd for and the old widow, *Mrs. Furioso* complains of Rogues; saying that she "can scarce keep a goose or a turkey in safety." They all drink to one another and soon the old lady cries: "Well, it is my bed-time; but my daughter will show you the way to yours, for I know you would willingly be in it."

Valentine is invited to eat supper with *Florida,* but he says he has no stomach for it. (He is love-sick). He invites *Mrs. Furiosa* and *Florida* to visit his *Mother's* house; which invitation they accept. The following scene shows the House-keeper, *Favourite,* preparing the repast:

Fav.: Mistress, shall I put Mushrooms, Mangoes, or Bamboons into the Sallad?

LadyB.: Yes, I pr'ythee, the best thou hast.

Fav.: Shall I use Ketchop or Anchovies in the Gravy?

Lady B.: What you will.

A *Mrs. Candia* enters and wishes to make a present of a Hawk to *Valentine. Florida,* his new sweetheart, grows jealous and resolves to leave him and run away with an odd sort of fellow, one *Major Sly. Valentine,* to appease her, sends her a message by his *Boy-Servant,* with some Tokens of his Distress; to wit: the Hawk, "torn to pieces by his own hands." (The Hawk, being too valuable to destroy, he used, instead, the wings and legs of a Fowl). The beautiful *Florida* refuses to be pacified and the Quarrel continues. *Valentine* suddenly decides to brush-off and he departs for the Wilderness where he may grieve in Solitude. However, he and his servant make scant provision for their departure, and in the fourth act we find Valentine in the most miserable condition that the Joint Arts of Cookery and Poetry are able to represent.

There is a scene of the greatest Horror and most moving to Compassion of anything that I have seen among the moderns; for here we behold an innocent young man, who has both lost his sweetheart and left his house before supper was to be served. *Valentine* and the *Boy* come to a grove of confused trees where an Owl halloos, whilst a Bear and a Leopard walk across the Desert in the background. *Valentine* takes refuge in a Hollow Tree, and converses with his boy, as follows:

Boy: There is nothing left in the wallet but one piece of cheese. What shall we do for bread?

Val.: When we have slept we shall seek out some roots.

Boy: And for drink, Master—what shall we do for drink?

Val.: Under that rock a Spring of pure water I see—it will refresh our thirst.

This heart-rending scene closes the Third Act, and it is dismal for the Audience to consider how *Valentine* and the *Boy* (who seems to have an eager stomach) should continue there, in a starving condition, whilst the musitians are playing the latest minuets and jigs.

A theatrical device called Catastrophe is now imployed for the Fourth Act. *Valentine* has grown a long beard and has become very weak with fasting during his sojourn in the Hollow Tree; he sends a message to *Florida,* saying that he is about to expire without her love. She quickly enters and embraces him, admitting that she has doubtless offended him too much, but that she will attend him home, cherish him with cordialls; make him wholesome broths, and be a tender nurse to him. Valentine's *Mother* orders the best entertainment that can be provided, and to get all ready for a happy ending, which consists of a Wedding supper and a Dance in the Fifth and final Act.

Now, some Persons admire meagre Tragedies, but give me a Play where there is a Prospect of Good Meat or Good Wine in every act, and where Love has a Happy Conclusion.

FOOD FOR THOUGHT

"Does not our life consist of the Four Elements?" asked Sir Toby Belch.

"Fayth, so they say," said Sir Andrew Aguecheek, "but I rather think it consists of eating and drinking."

There is many a man whose love has resulted from a full stomach, for a good meal has a marvellous effect on the heart. A learned Frenchman once remarked that it is wise to marry your cook rather than lose her, and many happily married men have followed this advice. A good cook needs few other virtues; she needs no tuneable voice to sing him madrigals, no gentle lute to play him ditties. She has even no need of fancie gownes or sweet scents, for who will deny that the aroma of good beef simmering in the pott with onions and herbs surpasses any other exotic perfume?

The ancient Egyptians knew little of the Art of Cookery. Cleopatra had no great mind to content Antony with such pleasures (though 'tis sayd she had others) for she was unable, when he came in, to make him a glass of small beer; nor had she an Orange or a Lemon to her veal; nay, not even rose-water to her codlings. The Romans, you will remember, had for years been accustomed to such delicacies.

Apicius commended Brawn as most delicious with a sauce of mustard and honey. Sauced Hogs' Feet, Cheeks and Eares were a delicacie, he tells us, not

Ariel Hall

serv'd onlie at Christmas. Fish was marinated, then fried in oil; and the moment they were taken up, boiling vinegar was thrown upon them. Apicius had also a way of mincing herbs with oil and salt and then boiling them. The green Asparagus was a great care of ancient Gardeners; Cucumbers were pared and boiled with oil, vinegar and honey. Boiled Cabbage was always a first course, because quantities of wine could afterwards be consumed with no disturbance.

For a sumptuous and costlie banquet, nothing exceeded Hog-Meat. It was so esteemed by the Romans that laws had to be made against its excessive use. But, Alas! the Degeneracy of our present usage is such that few besides the writer know of the excellence of a Virgin Sow, and know how to vary her into those fifty dishes which Pliny says were usually made of that delicious creature. Furthermore, Galen tells us that the fellow who eats Bacon for two or three days before he is tö box or wrestle, shall be much stronger than if he should eat the best Roast Beef or Bag Pudding in the parish.

But in the opinion of the Romans the most delicious animal was no other than that harmless creature, The Dormouse. Apicius devis'd an odd sort of Fate for these poor creatures—some to be bon'd; others to be put whole, with odd ingredients into Hogs-guts, and so, boil'd for Sausages. In ancient times, people made it their business to fatten them. Unfortunately, Bambouselbergius's "Treatise on Fattening Dormice" is lost. They were a common dish at great entertainments, and serv'd with Poppies and Honey, they made a soporiferous dainty—as good as Owl-pye to such as want a nap after dinner.

Happy were the Romans in great Examples, but the Britons have no need to repine. Herrings, Eel, Crabs and Lobster are here in great plenty. Of Mackarel there are such quantities that there is a public allowance for it. There is, in the markets, more Oxen than Garlick; Gray Peas in May are the delight of all people, and every night there goes by an old woman crying "Hot gray Peas and Bacon," which though delicious, I take to be too windy for supper meat, and am inclin'd to believe that hot ox-cheeks and wardens (pears) are wholesomer.

Onions will make even Heirs or Widows weep;
The tender lettuce brings on softer sleep;
Eat Beef or Pye-crust if you'd serious be;
Your Shell-Fish raises Venus from the Sea;
For Nature, that inclines to ill or good
Still nourishes our Passions by our Food.

To conclude a meal what could be finer than Hasty Pudding?

Ye Virgins, as these lines you kindly take,
So may you still such glorious Pudding make,
That crowds of Youth may ever be at strife
To gain the sweet Composer for his wife.

But if so be that you would try another sweet, there's nothing that can compare with Apple-Pye, for costly flavour, for outward beauty, or for inward taste. Add a few Quinces to your Pye, and perfect it with cream; adorn the brim with Crinkumcranks—and the pleased Spectator will greet each fresh Pye with virgin-fancies and new conceits.

Now, dear Reader, I have overstay'd my time; but if you will choose a dear Companion, I would invite you to a Roman dinner, of a few, but choice Dishes to cover the Table. These will be, unless you can think of something better: a Salacacaby, a Dishe of Fenugreek, a Wild Sheep's Head ,and appurtenance with a suitable Electuary, a Ragout of Capon's Stones and some Dormouse Sausages. These will satisfy a man's stomach and create his inner Happiness. For he who minds not his Belly will hardly be mindful of his other Pleasures.

(*Original Works,* by Dr. William King)

LOVE IS LIKE WAR

Love, an' please your honour, is exactly like war, in this; that a soldier, though he has escaped three weeks complete o' Saturday night,—may nevertheless be shot through his heart on Sunday morning— it happened so here, an' please your honour, with this difference only—that it was on Sunday in the afternoon, when I fell in love all at once—. It burst upon me, an' please your honour, like a bomb—scarce giving me time to say, "God bless me."

I thought, Trim, said my uncle Toby, a man never fell in love so very suddenly.

Yes, an' please your honour, if he is in the way of it—replied Trim.

I prithee, quoth my uncle Toby, inform me how this matter happened.

—With all pleasure, said the corporal, making a bow.

It was on a Sunday, in the afternoon—

Everything was still and hush as midnight about the house—

—When the fair Beguine came in to see me.

My wound was then in a fair way of doing well—the inflammation had been gone off for some time, but it was succeeded with an itching both above and below my knee, so insufferable, that I had not shut my eyes the whole night for it.

Let me see it, said she, kneeling down upon the

"Love is exactly like war . . ."

ground—it only wants rubbing a little; so, covering it with the bed-clothes, she began with the fore-finger of her right hand to rub under my knee, guiding her fore-finger backwards and forwards by the edge of the flannel which kept on the dressing.

In five or six minutes I felt slightly the end of her second finger—then her third and her fourth—she continued rubbing in that way for a good while; it then came into my head that I should fall in love—I blushed when I saw how white a hand she had.

The fair Beguine, said the corporal, continued rubbing with her whole hand under my knee—till I feared her zeal would weary her—"I would do a thousand times more," said she, "for the love of Christ"—in saying which, she passed her hand across the flannel, to the part above my knee, which I had equally complained of, and rubbed it also.

I perceived then, I was beginning to be in love—

As she continued rub-rub-rubbing—I felt it spread from under her hand—to every part of my frame—.

The more she rubbed, and the longer strokes she took—the more the fire kindled in my veins—till at length, by two or three strokes longer than the rest—my passion rose to the highest pitch—I seized her hand—and then thou clapped'st it to thy lips, Trim, said my uncle Toby—and madest a speech.

Whether the corporal's amour terminated precisely in the way my uncle Toby described it, is not material; it is enough that it contained in it the essence of all the love romances which have ever been wrote since the beginning of the world.

(*Life & Opinions of Tristram Shandy, Gent.*
by Laurence Sterne)

A POEM ON LOVE, AS RECITED BY THE MONKEY ON THE FIRST DAY OF SPRING

A POEM ON LOVE AND MARRIAGE,
AS RECITED BY THE MONKEY

Once a yeär, on the twentieth of March, all the Beastes and Birdes of the forest gather for the Great Event: The recitation by the Monkey, of his famous alphabeticall Poem on Love and Marriage. This had been handed down from generation to generation, and was consider'd the *ne plus ultra* of Wisdom. This is how it goes:

A. Ask not for Love—but give it;
Act as you would have things be.
Such advice my Mother gave, and so I give to Thee.

B. Better to have lov'd and lost, than never to have lov'd at all.
These, from a wise man, are words that I recall.

C. Consent to Life. Reach out like a Tree
to all things, great and small.
This wisdom is a gift to you, from me.

D. Do not depend on anyone, but speak Devotion
to thy mate, with Deeds unselfish,

E. Enduring love needs endless Kindness
even more than Passion.

F. Forget not Fun and Friendship; mix well that dish
if thou would'st have love's fruit,
but taste with caution.

G. Gauge thy chances; Guard thy charms;
Give thy pleasures to one lover's arms.

H. Happiness comes to those who now possess it,
So haste not, nor hurry;
Treasure every hour and minute.

I. Indeed, it is said that 'Better a good Mate
than Rubies—but there be many imitations
So 'tis wise to wait. Every man and woman too
has Limitations.

J. Joined together for better, or for worse
'Tis thine to make of Marriage Joy or Curse.
(A Marriage of true Minds is Heaven on Earth,
See that thou appreciat'st of what is thine, the
worth.)

K. Keep the Kindness and the Ways
That were practiced in olden Days
The kind of Manners known in days of yore
When Knighthood was in Flow'r.

L. Loveliness is the Secret to Love's maze
So be lovelie in thy Ways.

M. Matrimony is a state of great Import
Mind the Money, the Manners and the Meals
See that thy Morals be of good report
Think, before you act, of how another feels.

N. Nor loose thy Tongue without a thought
Of how't affects another.
No hurt is greater than a word unkind
Stop, Look, Listen, even though 'tis true that
love is blind.

O. Offer sweet scent to thy mate
Cleanliness is next to Godliness 'tis said.
Odours furnish much to Love or Hate
Such small things may keep you single, or
happ'ly wed.

P. Perfection exists only in Heav'n, not on Earth
Neither you nor I can be a Perfect better-half.
Have Patience inexhaustible. Find the mirth in all things.
Scold not. Wait 'til you can laugh.
(Nothing in the world matters very much.
Children, Dogs, Men—All answer to the gentle touch.)

Q. Question not thy Friend, if asking makes things worse
Quietness takes from Misunderstanding, its curse.

R. Reciprocal Regard and Respect is the Wise Advice
Given my by a man who never married twice.
and

S. Sweetness, Simplicity and Serenity for the She
Who would an ador'd woman be.

T. Theories come and theories go
But you get Roses if you plant them
And if you fail to use a Hoe
Weeds also grow.

U. Under no circumstances forget to say
Not "I"—but "We",
To think, not "Mine"—but "Ours."

V. Victory in love comes to those
Who plant the proper flowers.

W. When you find a good thing, don't look for a better; but beware a

X. Xanthippe for Mate.

Y. You, Yourself are the soil to cultivate
And to love is always better than to hate.

Z. Zones of Love are like the weather
Two sunny days come seldom twice together.
Now hot, now cold; now Fair, now Stormy;
Now Rain, Now Snow,—now Intervals of Sun
And so it ever was since Time begun.

The Moral of my Tale
is easy to recall.
The Zenith of Life
is
Love—for All.

And so...
Good Night to you here,
and Good Morrow hereafter

Since this love will conquer one by one,
Let's all agree to yield; the work is done.

BIBLIOGRAPHY

The Geneva Bible (1560)
Aesop's Fables
Three Ladies of London (1584)
Vulgar Errors by Sir Thomas Browne d. 1682
The Court of Elizabeth by L. Aikin
Advice to Lovers by R. W. (1680)
Lives of Eminent Men by John Aubrey, Esq. 1625-1697
British Essayists: *The Spectator Papers. Connoisseur, The Guardian Col. & Thorne, The World*
Illustrations of Old English Literature by J. P. Collier
Original Works by Dr. William King, L.L.D. (d. 1712)
Harleian Miscellanies Vol. IX, X, & XII
The Percy Anecdotes
The Works of John Dryden Book II, Eleg. 19
Crums fal'n from King James' Table, gather'd by Sir Thomas Overbury
Comments on Corpulency by William Wadd
Unpublished Ms. (coll. F. G. Hall)

This first edition of *Pills to Purge the Paines of Love* by Ariel Hall is set in Baskerville type, and the paper is Superfine Text. The edition is limited to 600 copies, of which only 500 copies are for sale.

This is number 459

Ariel Hall